The Motorist's Guide to Parking Tickets

"Parking enforcement under local authority control is now used as a vehicle to generate ever increasing income levels. It has long since ceased to be parking control designed to promote the free flow of traffic, enhance the safety of other road users and pedestrians, and is now an easy way for members in some authorities to increase cash flow."

Paul Sale, parking control manager, London Borough of Barnet, June 2003.

The Motorist's Guide to Parking Tickets

John Squires

Copyright © 2004 John Squires

The moral right of the author has been asserted.

Apart from any fair dealing for the purposes of research or private study, or criticism or review, as permitted under the Copyright, Designs and Patents Act 1988, this publication may only be reproduced, stored or transmitted, in any form or by any means, with the prior permission in writing of the publishers, or in the case of reprographic reproduction in accordance with the terms of licences issued by the Copyright Licensing Agency. Enquiries concerning reproduction outside those terms should be sent to the publishers.

Matador
9 De Montfort Mews
Leicester LE1 7FW, UK
Tel: (+44) 116 255 9311
Email: books@troubador.co.uk
Web: www.troubador.co.uk

ISBN 1 904744 21 4

Typesetting: Troubador Publishing Ltd, Leicester, UK
Printed and bound by Cromwell Press Ltd, Trowbridge, Wilts

Matador is an imprint of Troubador Publishing Ltd

Contents

Contents

Foreword

Many councils have now taken over parking enforcement from the police in what is known as 'decriminalised' enforcement. From the start there were complaints, which councils denied, that they were 'policing for profit'. However, in 2003 one council admitted that its parking enforcement contractor was offering incentives in the form of a car, widescreen TV and holiday vouchers to its 'best' parking attendants. Several other councils have been found guilty of acting illegally with councils and parking attendants 'cutting legal corners', proving that there really is a dash for cash.

For those that challenge incorrectly or unfairly issued tickets the standard of handling of representations by some councils often leaves a lot to be desired. Having had their representation rejected a significant proportion of motorists give up when, in fact, they may have well founded grounds for contesting liability.

This book explains the regulations and exemptions and will help prevent motorists from getting tickets in the first place. For those who think that they have received tickets incorrectly, it gives advice on how to challenge them.

Although advice is available from a number of sources this book draws them together and explains the intricacies of the system in layman's language. I hope that it will encourage more motorists to pursue their cases to adjudication.

Paul Watters
Head of Roads and Transport Policy
The AA Motoring Trust
Farnborough
Hampshire
GU14 0JW

Author's Preface

Hundreds of people seek advice on how to challenge parking tickets from the website *www.parkingticket.co.uk* every week. Although the site is helpful in assisting motorists to challenge unfairly or incorrectly issued parking tickets, few have access to the web when they return to their car to find that they have been ticketed. This book serves as a handy reference that can be kept in the car for such eventualities, and details the information that should be collected before leaving the location.

Parking enforcement is an expensive operation and councils are required to, at least, cover their costs. Their income is derived from paid-for parking and fines. It is no surprise that, as judge and jury when considering motorists' representations, they will be unwilling to concede points and will put pressure on motorists to pay-up. Some councils have even suggested that motorists taking their cases to adjudication could incur costs if they lose.

To be enforceable, restrictions must be correctly

lined and signed. However, few councils feel constrained in issuing tickets where lines are poorly maintained and signs are missing. Every year many thousands of motorists pay parking tickets that were issued to them in such circumstances. Others, unsure of their ground, pay because they don't think they have a good enough case to win an appeal. Armed with the information in this book you need not be one of them!

John Squires
parkdoc@parkingticket.co.uk
March 2004

Introduction

Many motorists take the view that, having paid their road tax, they are entitled to park in any street that does not have waiting restrictions. However, the only right anyone actually has on the public highway is to 'pass and repass.'

Parking controls are introduced for a number of reasons. Most importantly, on major roads, they keep the road clear thereby improving traffic flows. They also allow pedestrians and vehicles emerging from junctions to see and be seen. It is an offence to obstruct the highway without reasonable excuse. Indeed willful obstruction of the highway is an arrestable offence. But because obstruction is not a clear-cut offence, traffic regulation orders are used to make the situation clear and to provide a lesser offence enforced with a parking ticket.

Parking milestones

1930 Waiting restrictions appeared in London in the Piccadilly area.

Most people assume that 'parking' is a post-war phenomenon. However, in 1776 in Dorchester you could have been fined five shillings (25p – a considerable sum in those days!) for leaving a horse and cart longer than was necessary for loading and unloading.

1935	The parking meter was first used in Oklahoma
1956	Yellow lines were laid in Putney High Street
1958	Parking meters introduced in Mayfair
1959	The first residents' parking scheme introduced in Westminster
1960	Traffic warden service introduced
1993	Decriminalised enforcement under the Road Traffic Act 1991 started in Wandsworth
1994	Decriminalised enforcement started in the rest of London.
1996	Winchester city council became the first council outside London to introduce decriminalised enforcement

Although legal orders creating parking restrictions are made by highway authorities (county or borough councils), enforcement was traditionally the responsibility of the police. But parking enforcement never rated very high on the police's scale of priorities. Although traffic wardens were created to take on this responsibility, they were never at the required strength to adequately enforce the restrictions in force during the 1970s and 80s. With increasing car ownership and the associated parking problems, councils were under pressure to introduce more parking controls. These were resisted by the police. Clearly, if enforcement of existing restrictions was inadequate, additional restrictions would simply mean that the available resources would be spread even more sparsely.

An acceptance of the inadequacies of police enforcement, together with the need for additional parking controls, resulted in the Road Traffic Act 1991. This decriminalised parking offences and enabled councils to carry out their own parking enforcement. Parking fines became a civil debt and income from parking tickets was kept by the councils to help finance their enforcement operations.

The number of tickets issued by the London councils in the first full year of operation was almost twice as many as issued by police traffic wardens during the last year they carried out enforcement. This lead to accusations of councils 'policing for profit'.

The first person to receive a parking ticket from a traffic warden was Dr Thomas Creighton on 19 September 1960. He had parked his Ford Popular car outside a West End hotel to visit a patient suffering from a heart attack. However such was the outcry in the press over the ticket that it was cancelled!

Take up of decriminalised parking enforcement outside London has been slow. This is because set-up costs are high and smaller towns often do not have sufficient waiting restrictions to enable an enforcement operation to be financially viable. However, since parking enforcement does not figure on Home Office police targets for constabularies, more forces are giving notice that they no longer intend to carry out this function. It would appear that those provincial authorities that do not 'jump' will eventually be 'pushed' into carrying out their own enforcement.

Because Scottish law is different from the rest of the UK the appeals procedure differs slightly and it is not possible to make a Statutory Declaration. In Ireland there are no traffic regulation orders and enforcement is carried out on the basis of failing to comply with traffic signs.

What to do if you get a parking ticket

The only way you can guarantee not to get a parking ticket is to never have a motor vehicle! Parking attendants sometimes make a mistake in taking down a number – that mistaken number could be yours. Your car may have a clone – someone else is getting the tickets but you are getting the notices to owner.

Not all tickets are correctly issued. If you want to challenge one that you think has been unfairly or incorrectly issued, it is essential that you collect as much evidence as possible before you leave the location.

Most people do not see the parking attendant or traffic warden who issued the ticket. If you do return to your vehicle just as the ticket is being put under your wiper blade don't hurl abuse at the enforcement officer! This is counter productive as a ticket cannot be cancelled once it has been issued or is in the process of being issued. You would be far better off to enquire why it was issued and to point out why you think that it should not have been. If any points are conceded ask that they be noted in the officer's pocket book.

Check the ticket

The first thing to check is that the following details have been correctly recorded on the ticket:

1. *Vehicle registration number* (if this is wrong you can forget about the ticket because the DVLA enquiry will not return your particulars!)
2. *Location* – street and position in the street (e.g. outside 25 High Street).
3. *Date*.
4. *Time*(s) (e.g. 'at' or 'from/to').
5. *Contravention code*.
6. *Make of vehicle*.
7. *Colour of vehicle* (allow some latitude – 'metallic gold' might be described as brown!).
8. *Attendant's number*.
9. *Attendant's signature* (don't expect more than a squiggle!).

(See also 'Validity of Penalty Charge Notices' in the Key Cases section.)

who had reasonable cause to believe that the following parking contravention had occured: **83**

PARKED IN A PAY AND DISPLAY CAR PARK WITHOUT CLEARLY DISPLAYING A VALID PAY AND DISPLAY TICKET

You are therefore required to pay the sum of **£ 60.00** within 28 days. The charge will be reduced to £ **30.00** if payment is received within 14 days.

Issued by National Car Parks Limited on behalf of Bury MBC

This PCN says "You are therefore required to pay..." But "you" may not have to pay if you are not the owner of the vehicle.

Collect evidence

Nowadays many towns have controlled parking zones (CPZs). This is an area within which there is a common waiting restriction, say 8 a.m. to 6.30 p.m. Mondays to Saturdays. The operational hours of the CPZ are displayed on signs placed on both sides of the road at every point of entry to the zone. There are no signs to indicate the operational hours of the yellow lines within the zone except where restrictions differ from the zone times.

If you *are* in a CPZ:

1. Was there an entry sign on both sides of the road when you entered?
2. are the signs within the CPZ (at the location in question) facing towards the road?
3. Are any signs (at the location in question) faded, or obscured by foliage, making them difficult to read?
4. Within a parking bay there should be:
   - one sign, centrally located, if the bay is up to 30 metres in length (approximately five cars' length)
   - signs approximately 5 metres from each end and at a maximum spacing of 30 metres within the bay if it is over 30 metres in length.
5. Are lines missing or in poor condition?

If you are *not* in a CPZ:

1. Is there a sign on every lamp column?
2. Are signs no greater than 60 metres apart? (approximately 12 cars' length).
3. Are the signs facing towards the road?
4. Are any signs faded or obscured by foliage making them difficult to read?
5. Do all the signs have the same information? (if there is a change in the restriction there

should be a 'splitter' sign to that effect – see below)

To record evidence, a camera is invaluable. Disposable cameras with a flash can be purchased for under £10. Motorists should keep one in their vehicle as it could repay the investment many times over. If you don't have a camera then make a note of any defects that you find. For example, 'No sign on lamp column outside No. 5 The Avenue'. If you find any of these defects then you are in a stronger position to get the ticket cancelled.

A splitter sign.

Representations and appeals

If you receive a ticket from a police officer or a traffic warden you may challenge it by writing to the issuing constabulary or ticket office. If you present a strong case they may cancel the ticket. Otherwise they will say that, if you want to challenge it, you must argue your case in the magistrates' court.

Under decriminalised enforcement used by councils, there are two stages to challenging a ticket. Firstly a representation is made to the council. If your representation is rejected, and you are not satisfied with the council's reasons for the rejection, you may then appeal to an independent adjudicator.

Remember that you cannot pay and challenge a ticket. Receipt of payment automatically closes the case.

If you have grounds to challenge a ticket issued by a council you should do so as soon as possible. Although they are under no obligation to do so most councils will 'stop the clock' whilst they consider your initial representation. This means that even if they reject it they will still give you 14 days in which to pay at the reduced rate.

At this informal stage councils give only a cursory consideration of the representation and are likely to reject it in an attempt to encourage you to pay up at the discounted rate. Many people who are unsure of the strength of their case do so at this stage for fear of having to pay the full amount. If you get a standard reply that does not address the points that you raised, write back and ask them to address those specific points. However, the council may not be prepared to discuss the matter further until after they have served you a Notice to Owner (NtO). Once the NtO has been issued the full payment of the fine will be due if the representation and any subsequent appeal is unsuccessful.

The NtO is the formal document advising that you are the owner of a vehicle that, in the council's opinion, has parked in contravention of a restriction. You have 28 days from the date of the NtO to either pay the fine or make a formal representation to the council.

The council is obliged to deal with your representation 'fairly'. This means that it must also be timely in its replies. The longer it takes to reply and adequately answer your questions, the better the chance an adjudicator will be persuaded that the council has not treated you fairly and thus be more disposed to allow your appeal.

When rejecting a representation, councils must give a 'Notice of Rejection of Representations' (NoR). With this should be details of how to take the matter to appeal if you are not satisfied with the council's decision. You must either make an appeal or pay the fine within 28 days of receiving the NoR. Failure to do so will result in the council issuing a Charge Certificate and the fine being increased by 50%, without any further opportunity to appeal!

At first sight the grounds on which you may make an appeal look fairly narrow. They are if:

1. You were not the owner of the vehicle at the time of the contravention.
2. The vehicle had been taken without your consent at the time of the contravention.
3. You are a vehicle hire company.
4. The traffic regulation order was invalid.
5. The penalty exceeded the relevant amount.
6. The contravention did not occur.

The majority of appeals are on the grounds that 'the contravention did not occur.' If, for example, signs or lines are inadequate or missing then tickets should not be issued because the restriction is not enforceable – so 'the contravention did not occur'. By making an appeal you have the satisfaction of knowing that it will cost the council money to register it with the appeal service plus officer time putting its case together, assuming your appeal is challenged. Over 30% of appeals are not challenged by councils.

You can elect to appeal by post or attend in person. Councils are obliged to send copies of their evidence to you and the appeals service no later than three days before the date of the hearing. If the appeal service does not receive the evidence within the three day deadline then you will automatically win the appeal.

The adjudicator will have a copy of the PCN, the parking attendant's (PA's) notes and any evidence that you have submitted when making representations to the council. The most important document is the PCN and the adjudicator will check that all the details recorded by the PA are correct. Should any detail be wrong, illegible or missing, the PCN will be declared invalid and the appeal allowed.

The council must satisfy the adjudicator that all the facts necessary to establish the contravention have been proved. These include:

- the precise location of the vehicle

- that waiting was restricted at the location in question
- the restriction was properly indicated
- the PCN was issued

If the council fails in any respect the appeal will succeed without the appellant providing any evidence. For example, if a road is subject to different restrictions at different locations, no plan has been submitted by the council showing precisely where the vehicle was located and it is not possible to determine the location from the PA's notes, then the appeal will be allowed.

Each fact must be established on the 'balance of probabilities'. This is a much lower standard than 'beyond reasonable doubt', which applies in criminal law. Basically, the adjudicator needs to be satisfied that a fact is more likely to be true than not. Most of the evidence will be in the form of documentation although some facts cannot be proved by documents – it is not possible to provide a document to prove that a motorist did not find a ticket on the vehicle!

Adjudicators use their skill to weigh up the evidence and then decide which side of the line the balance of probabilities falls. It does not necessarily follow that evidence contained in a document will be preferred to oral or written statements. Indeed, the National Parking Appeals Service (NPAS) says that the power of oral evidence from an appellant who is patently honest should not be underestimated.

If you are unsuccessful in your appeal, you should pay the fine without delay as the adjudicator's decision is final and binding on both parties. In London, those who have lost a personal appeal can pay at the appeals centre. This facility may not be available in all appeal centres outside London in which case, as with refused postal appeals, you should pay the council in question. Failure to pay within 28 days will result in the council issuing a Charge Certificate and the debt being increased by 50%.

If the increased fine is not paid within 14 days of the date of the Charge Certificate, the debt will be registered. In England and Wales this will be at the Parking Enforcement Centre at Northampton County Court and a further £5 added to the debt. In Scotland if the debt is not paid within 14 days of the issue of the Charge Certificate the certificate then becomes the 'extract registered decree arbitral'. It has the same powers as a warrant and allows it to be passed to Sheriff's Officers for recovery. In England and Wales the issuing council will write to you, advising that the debt has been registered and enclosing a Statutory Declaration form. (Statutory Declarations do not apply under Scottish Law)

You must either pay the debt or make a Statutory Declaration. This is an oath by the person who has the debt registered against them. It can only be made on the grounds that:-

- you did not receive a NtO.
- you made formal representations to the council but did not receive a Notice of Rejection of Representation.
- you appealed to the parking adjudicator and had no response from the adjudication service.

A Statutory Declaration must be signed in the presence of a commissioner for oaths, an officer of the county court or a magistrate. There is no charge if your signature is witnessed in a county court. The declaration must be completed and returned to the Parking Enforcement Centre within 21 days. If you make a Statutory Declaration that you did not receive a NtO or Notice of Rejection of Representation the council may still send one, in which case the procedure starts again.

If you do not either pay the debt or make a Statutory Declaration within 21 days the council will apply to the court for a Warrant of Execution. This authorises the council to recover the unpaid parking penalties using bailiffs.

Bailiffs will add their charges to the outstanding debt, which will not be insignificant. If you are a tenant with nothing of value that could be seized and auctioned by the bailiffs then you have nothing much to fear from this process. On the other hand, if you are an owner occupier with items of value in your home and who might need a future credit reference, then a county court judgement will affect your credit rating and your valuables could be auctioned to recover the debt.

Costs

Taking a case to appeal involves your time and possibly some expense. What are the chances of obtaining costs if your appeal is allowed? Adjudicators can award costs to appellants or councils if either party acts 'frivolously, vexaciously or wholly unreasonably'. The award of costs is the exception rather than the rule. However, you should ask the adjudicator for costs if you think you have grounds.

The question of the awarding of costs is addressed in Regulation 12 of The Road Traffic (Parking Adjudicators) (London) Regulations 1993.

> 12. (1) The adjudicator shall not normally make an order awarding costs and expenses, but may, subject to paragraph (2) make such an order –
>
> (a) against a party (including an appellant who has withdrawn his appeal or a local authority that has consented to an appeal being allowed) if he is of the opinion that that party has acted frivolously or vexatiously or that his conduct in making, pursuing or resisting an appeal was wholly unreasonable; or
>
> (b) against the local authority, where it considers that the disputed decision was wholly unreasonable.
>
> (2) An order shall not be made under paragraph (1) against a party unless that party has been given an opportunity of making representations against the making of the order.
>
> (3) An order under paragraph (1) shall require the party against whom it is made to pay the other party a specified sum in respect of the costs and expenses incurred by that other party in connection with the proceedings.

The crucial points are the interpretation of the words 'frivolously', 'vexatiously' and 'wholly unreasonably.' According to my thesaurus, synonyms for 'frivolous' include:- trivial, petty, trifling and unimportant. 'Vexatious' – troublesome, distressing, grievous, harsh. 'Unreasonable' – inadequate, unfair, unjust, intolerable.

It would appear to me to be 'wholly unreasonable' if a council refused to cancel a PCN on a point of fact. For example, where evidence had been provided of loading/unloading taking place or where signs were either missing or inadequate.

Clamping and Removal

Getting a parking ticket is bad enough but being clamped or removed is far worse, as it means payment of a release fee in addition to the parking ticket. Councils may, at their discretion, clamp or remove any illegally parked vehicle. Their only constraint is that they must wait 15 minutes after the expiry of the time paid for at a meter or pay-and-display bay.

Some councils, like Manchester, have a priority list for removals but many others do not. The arbitrary way in which councils remove vehicles is of concern to the National Parking Appeals Service (NPAS). It compared the number of removals different councils carried out as a percentage of the total PCNs they issued.

In Oxfordshire this represented just 0.2%, in Manchester 4.15%, but in Bristol a massive 11.9%. Thus a motorist parking illegally in Bristol was almost 60 times more likely to be removed than one in Oxford! NPAS is concerned that appropriate local guidance is not in place and that, contrary to the Secretary of State's guidance, in some areas removals are carried out on an *ad hoc* basis.

The legislation permitting the clamping and removal of vehicles was introduced prior to 1991 while it was still the sole responsibility of the police. Unlike councils, there was no financial benefit to the police in clamping or removing vehicles so safeguards to prevent abuse were not necessary.

Because clamping and removal operations are expensive to set up and operate there is a suspicion that councils 'go shopping' for vehicles to keep the operation in the black. This will continue unless and until there is a change in the legislation to lay down criteria for when vehicles may be clamped or removed.

Before a vehicle is clamped or removed it must first be issued with a parking ticket. Although you have to pay the ticket with the release fee you can still challenge it provided that you do so within 28 days of its issue. If your challenge is successful you, of course, also get the release fee refunded. Councils are obliged to respond to your representation within 56 days of its receipt, failure to do so means that they must repay both the ticket and release fee.

Clamping on private land

Clamping on private land was declared illegal in Scotland but anybody, with the land owner's consent, can clamp vehicles on private land in England and Wales. Clampers charge exorbitant rates for the release of vehicles and, of course, will only accept payment in cash. By the end of 2004 it will be illegal for anyone to clamp on private land who is not licensed by the Security Industry Authority and operates within the Authority's strict code of practice. This should rein in the excesses of private clampers.

Private Parking Tickets

A number of organisations use management

companies to control their car parks and private access roads. Many of these management companies issue 'private' parking tickets to motorists who park 'illegally'. For a fee the DVLA will release keepers' details to any company that can demonstrate that it has 'reasonable cause for wanting the particulars'. Having obtained the keeper's details payment of a fine will then be demanded. If payment is not forthcoming the company would have to take out a private prosecution to pursue the matter.

The DVLA requires such companies abide by a voluntary code of practice. Companies must ensure that:

- adequate signing be displayed where enforcement activity is to be carried out
- notices giving full details of the parking contravention and the proposed course of action to be taken by the enforcer, including that their name and address will be requested from the DVLA, should be placed on the vehicle
- companies should not create the impression that action is being taken on behalf of a public body
- vehicle keepers must be contacted by letter and should not be approached in their homes

other than for the service of notices and court papers until a court judgment has been obtained

- enquiries must include details of the incident giving rise to the claim including date, time, vehicle registration number, make, model and colour

If you dispute the validity of the ticket and the company refuses to cancel it you would have to argue your case in court.

When can and can't you park here?

To sum up, your strategy with council issued tickets should be as follows:

1. Check the parking ticket to make sure all the details recorded are correct.
2. Collect as much evidence as possible before leaving the location
3. Challenge the ticket without delay.
4. If you have not had an acknowledgement within a couple of weeks or a reply within a month, write again enclosing a copy of your original letter. Ask them to acknowledge receipt and enquire when you will get a reply.
5. If you telephone, be sure to make a note of the name of the person you spoke to and what was said. (If who you spoke to concedes any of the points you raised, confirm those points by letter.)
6. If you receive an unsatisfactory reply, or one in the form of a standard letter of refusal, write again requesting answers to the specific points that you raised.
7. The council is likely to reject a 'initial representation' in the hope that you will pay at the reduced rate rather than risk failure later and have to pay the full amount. If you are sure of your ground don't be put off.
8. The more persistent you are, the better the chance that the council will concede the case.

However, if the council refuses to cancel the ticket, don't be put off as you can always take the matter to appeal. When rejecting a representation, councils must give a 'Notice of Rejection of Representations'. With this should be details of how to take the matter to appeal if you are not satisfied with the council's findings.

The restrictions

Waiting restrictions

Waiting restrictions are introduced where it is considered necessary to keep lengths of kerb-side clear of parked vehicles. This may be to maintain traffic flow along busy roads or to keep lines of vision clear for road safety reasons. Vehicles are exempted from waiting restrictions when:

- instructed to wait by a police constable in uniform
- stopping to avoid an accident
- broken down
- waiting whilst a barrier or gate is being opened
- taking in petrol, oil, water or air at the kerbside
- being used for fire brigade, police or ambulance purposes
- it is a military forces vehicle
- being used for road maintenance with the authority of a council

- being used for removal of an obstruction to traffic
- being used for the removal of furniture from adjacent premises
- being used for collection of postal packages from a post box or adjacent premises
- selling goods from a pitch, from a vehicle holding a licence from a council
- it is a bus setting down or picking up passengers
- waiting to allow a person to board or alight a vehicle and load or unload any personal luggage
- loading or unloading goods
- displaying a disabled person's badge and clock

Waiting restrictions are indicated by signs and yellow lines. Double yellow lines always mean no waiting at any time. Single yellow lines apply where the restriction is less than 'At any time'. This means that the restriction could be between one and 23 hours a day.

Until the end of 1998 single yellow lines rarely applied on Sundays. With the advent of Sunday trading, single yellow lines that also apply on Sundays are becoming more common. The majority of single yellow lines still only apply Monday to Saturday and, because of this, motorists frequently get penalised on Sundays for parking on single lines that do apply. Therefore, you must always check the signs when you encounter single yellow lines.

Since March 2002 signs are no longer required for double yellow lines, but for a restriction less than 'At any time' there must be both a single yellow line and a sign to indicate the operating hours.

Signs

There must be a sign on every lamp column along the length of single yellow line restriction. Additionally there must be a sign within 15 metres of the termination points of the restriction. As restrictions tend to abut one another in urban areas there should be a 'splitter sign' (with arrows) indicating where one restriction ends and another starts. If there are either no lamp columns, or they are spaced more than 60 metres apart, then supplementary posts must be erected to mount the signs on. Most urban and suburban areas have lamp columns spaced at intervals considerably less than 60 metres but it is not unusual for councils to also erect posts between lamp columns.

The only exception to this is within a controlled parking zone (CPZ). CPZs have their hours of operation displayed at each entry point to the zone. Only restrictions that are not the same as the CPZ hours will be signed. (With the exception of 'At any time') If you miss the entry signs, and many drivers do, it is fairly safe to say that where you see permit or meter parking bays you are within a CPZ.

If a zone entry sign is missing or, as here, obscured by a forest of signs there are grounds for challenging tickets issued within the zone.

Lines

The yellow lines must be marked along the extent of the restriction and have a 'T-bar' at the point of termination. There is also a requirement for a T-bar where restrictions change from a single to a double yellow line, and *vice versa*.

Bill Robson, a retired photographer from Ripon in North Yorkshire, became something of a local celebrity in 2001 when he successfully challenged a parking ticket on the grounds that the yellow line in question had no T-bar and, therefore, did not comply with the regulations. He subsequently photographed dozens of locations where the T-bars were missing and presented them to North Yorkshire police. As a result the police suspended enforcement until the council surveyed all the lines and rectified the defects.

At first sight it would appear that if a ticketed motorist was to take the trouble to follow the yellow line to its termination point and find that the T-bar was missing, the ticket would have to be cancelled. However, there are several factors that make this a less than clear cut issue:

- the missing T-bar may be round a corner in a side street – would this render the line in the main road invalid or only the length relating to the side street?

- the restriction may abut another restriction meaning that no T-bar is required. (unless the change is from a single to a double yellow line or vice versa)
- T-bars are also not required where a yellow line meets a pedestrian crossing or a permitted parking bay.
- the further that the missing T-bar is from the point where the ticket was issued the weaker becomes the case that it is relevant in determining the validity of the parking ticket.

That said, it is always worth while checking whether there is a T-bar.

Road lines are, with very few exceptions, marked with a material called thermoplastic. As the name implies it is a plastic material which, when heated, melts to become a viscous slurry. Apart from being more durable than paint it has the added advantage that when it comes into contact with the road it solidifies almost immediately, allowing traffic to pass over it within seconds of being laid. However, it will not adhere to the road surface in wet conditions and will quickly break up if the road surface is in poor condition.

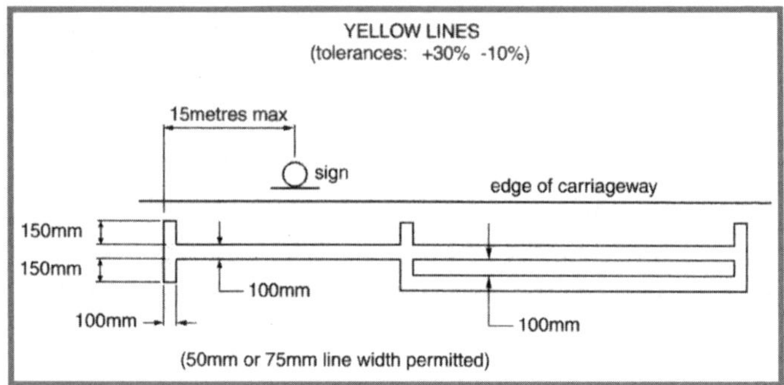

Yellow line and T-bar dimensions.

Enforcement is not possible if a line is either missing or not clearly marked. However, the point at which a line becomes 'unclear' is a matter for debate. For this reason, photographic evidence is invaluable if you intend to challenge a ticket on the grounds that the line was not clear.

Loading restrictions

Loading restrictions are introduced where it is essential to maintain traffic flows along busy roads and at locations where a waiting vehicle would obstruct the passage of other vehicles, or be a hazard to pedestrians. Blue Badge holders must not park where loading restrictions are in operation, apart from that the same exemptions apply as for waiting restrictions.

Loading restrictions are indicated by signs and yellow stripes or 'blips' on the kerb or side of the road. Double blips mean 'At any time' and single blips anything less than 'At any time'.

It is not practicable to mark thermoplastic on kerb stones so road paint is used instead. The passage of feet means that the blips need remarking more frequently than lines. With the maintenance problem in mind, 'At any time' loading restrictions must be signed, but this does not absolve councils from the responsibility to maintain blips.

Stopping restrictions

At some locations it is illegal even to stop unless directed to do so by a police constable. These are commonly rural clearways (trunk roads) but can also be on fly-overs where a stationary vehicle would cause obstruction and delay. Rural clearways do not have yellow lines or other carriageway markings to support the No Stopping signs. Stopping is also prohibited on some bus stops and school entrance markings.

Exemptions are similar to those for waiting and loading and unloading but do not include stopping to allow passengers to be set down or picked up, or the loading or unloading of goods or baggage.

Bus Stops

Common sense and courtesy would suggest that motorists should not park at bus stops. However, both these qualities being in ever shorter supply, councils have traditionally made Bus Stop Clearway Orders to prohibit stopping at bus stops. These were marked with a yellow 'cage' with the words 'BUS STOP' and a sign. However, with effect from April 2003, the requirement to make an Order ceased. Now enforcement of bus stop clearways may be carried out regardless of whether the clearway in question is the subject of an Order.

Exemptions are as for stopping restrictions.

Footways

As a rule of thumb, carriageways are for vehicles and footways are for pedestrians. Indeed, within the strict interpretation of the law, it is even illegal for anyone to push a buggy along a footway! The legal situation with regard to parking with one or more wheels on the footway is different in London to the rest of the country. In London, the Greater London Council made an order in 1974 which made it illegal to park with wheels on any footway in Greater London except where there are signs indicating that it is expressly permitted. In the rest of the country the reverse is the situation; you may park with wheels on the footway

Markings indicating the permitted limit of encroachment on the footway.

unless there are signs indicating that it is expressly forbidden.

Night Lorry Ban

In certain towns and cities it is illegal to park a commercial vehicle over a specified weight overnight. In London this weight is five tonnes gross vehicle weight. The restriction is indicated on entry signs at all entrances to the restricted area rather like a CPZ. Unlike a CPZ there are also 'repeater' signs and there should be at least one in each street.

Councils are in a no-win situation when it comes to trying to balance the needs of pedestrians, residents and motorists. The matter is further complicated by the fact that motorists can also be residents and pedestrians and opinion changes according to the circumstances.

Motorists want major roads kept clear so that their journeys are not delayed due to congestion but expect a couple of minutes grace if they want to stop on a yellow line. On arriving home they want to be able to park, preferably outside their own home, and are aggrieved if there are no free spaces; particularly if the road is parked up by non-residents.

Permitted Parking

Permitted parking is the generic term for all the places where you may park, e.g. meter bays, pay-and-display bays, permit holder bays, etc.

Meter bays

Parking meters were the original means of collecting money for kerb-side parking. For a variety of reasons they have, to a large extent, been superseded by pay-and-display machines. However, there are still quite a few around.

The advantage of meters, from the motorist's point of view, is that there is one per bay so there is no need to go in search of a pay-and-display machine to buy a ticket. A disadvantage is that they usually only accept one or two different coin types so you must have the correct change. Payment is due the moment the vehicle is parked; there is no grace period allowed to 'go for change.'

The timing mechanism is either mechanical (clockwork) or electronic. When coins are inserted the meter displays the time paid for and starts counting down. When the time expires the meter indicates 'Penalty' and if the vehicle remains it is liable to be ticketed.

In 2001 the Sunday Times randomly tested the timing accuracy of 95 parking meters in London, Salford, Southend, Doncaster, Newcastle and Edinburgh. They found that 19 were fast by up to nine minutes in the hour and another seven swallowed coins without registering any credit.

Interestingly, councils are required to check and log malfunctions of meters under the provisions of the Road Traffic Regulation Act 1984 Section 46(3) which says:

Where provision is made for the use of parking meters it shall be the duty of the local authority to take such steps as appear to be appropriate for the periodical inspection of the meters and for the dealing with any found to be out of order; for securing the testing of the meters, both before they are brought into force and afterwards; and for recording the date on which and the person by whom a meter has been tested.

If you return to a meter bay shortly after the time has expired to find you have been ticketed it would be a good idea to write to the issuing authority and ask them for a copy of the record for when the meter was tested for accuracy under the terms of Section 46(3) of the Road Traffic Regulation Act 1984!

Multi-bay meters

Multi-bay meters are something between the traditional parking meter and pay-and-display. They control a number of parking bays – typically up to six. Each bay has its number indicated on the kerbside and the motorist has to ensure that payment is made for the correct bay as no ticket is issued.

Pay-and-display

Pay-and-display is the most common method of paying for parking. Up to two dozen bays can be served by a single machine. The guidance given to councils says that there should be a machine within sight of any given bay and be no further than 30 metres away.

From a motorist's point of view, pay-and-display

Multibay meter.

has an advantage over meters in that most denominations of coins are accepted. Some also accept credit cards and there are even some areas where payment by mobile phone is possible. Disadvantages are that no change is given and there is also a requirement to 'display' the ticket. This means that if you stick it to your windscreen and it falls off you are liable to get a parking ticket for 'failing to display a valid ticket'. For this rea-

Multibay meter numbers on footway.

son, I always recommend that tickets are placed face up on the dashboard on the side of the vehicle nearest the kerb.

As with meters, there is no grace period in which to go in search of change, and technically the vehicle is illegally parked from the moment you get out of your car until you return with the ticket. Common sense dictates that you will be away

Some councils expect motorists to go to extraordinary lengths to get a ticket!

from your car for a minute or two before you can purchase and display the ticket. However, more than a couple of minutes and you are increasingly liable to be ticketed.

If the first machine does not work, you will have to seek out another. If it's further up the street, fine, but keep your vehicle under observation so you can return to it immediately if necessary. Obviously, if you turn a corner to seek a machine just as a parking attendant enters the street then a ticket may have been issued before you return and you will have the hassle of writing in to try and get it cancelled. My advice, in such circumstances, would be to drive your car to a machine that is working and park there.

If a machine is out of order you must obtain a ticket from the next available machine.

Vouchers

This system involves pre-purchasing vouchers and validating them by indicating the date and time of arrival, usually by means of scratching off the appropriate panels. The voucher is then displayed in the same way as a pay-and-display ticket. The voucher system is very popular in Scandinavia, Israel, Ireland and Jersey.

Vouchers are a low cost, low-tech, cashless solution to the collection of parking tariffs and they avoid the cost and visual intrusion of pay-and-display machines or meters. For all that they have never really caught on in the UK.

Vouchers are usually sold at the sort of independent retail outlets that sell phone cards and lottery tickets. Herein lies part of the problem for councils. Traders are in a position to hold the council to ransom if they don't like some aspect of the parking scheme and will often refuse to sell vouchers if they are against the introduction of a parking scheme.

Furthermore, some motorists object to having to pre-pay for their parking, while for someone unfamiliar with an area there is the problem of not knowing where to go to purchase vouchers. Yet another problem is that a surprising number of motorists don't know what the date is – even though vouchers invariably have a calendar on the back!

Permit Holders

Within CPZs, a considerable amount of space will be for 'permit holders only'. This usually means residents but could also include business permit holders. Sometimes bays are created for shared-use, which means they can be used either by permit holders or by someone who buys a ticket from a pay-and-display machine. Shared-use bays avoid the situation where pay-and-display bays could be full and spaces remain in permit holder only bays or *vice versa*.

With permitted parking bays the advice, as ever, is to check the signs before parking. The sign will indicate the category of user permitted to use the bay and the hours of operation. Be careful – permitted parking bays sometimes operate longer than the hours of the waiting restrictions operating in the CPZ.

If the bay is less than 30 metres in length (six car lengths or less) there must be a sign located some-

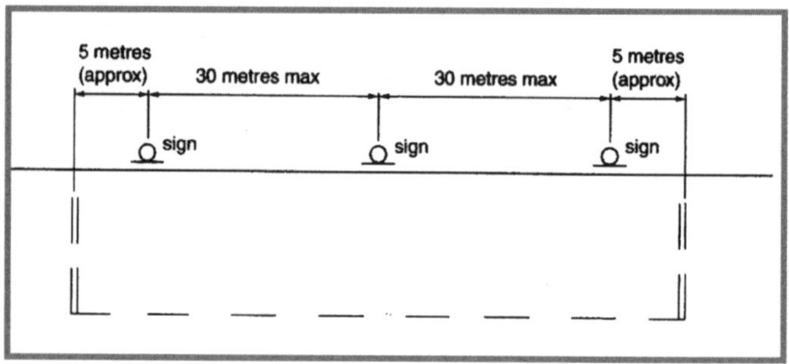

Parking bay over 30 metres in length.

where towards its centre. If the bay is longer than 30 metres then there must be signs 'approximately' five metres from each end and further signs spaced at no greater than 30 metre intervals along its length. Therefore you should never be more than 15 metres (approximately three cars' length) from a sign.

Solo Motorcycle Bays

Within CPZs space is sometimes allocated for solo motorcycles. The bays are marked with the words 'SOLO MOTORCYCLES ONLY'. There are no accompanying signs. It would not be unreasonable to assume that this type of bay is only enforceable during the operational hours of the CPZ.

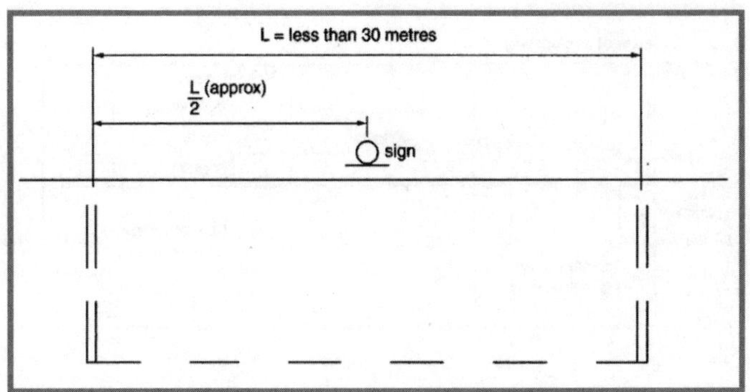

Parking bay under 30 metres in length.

However, they apply 'At any time' so don't ever park a car in one – especially in Croydon – as you could get a parking ticket.

Some councils allow motorcycles to park in permit holders' bays but there is no way of knowing this from the signs. To find out it is necessary to contact the council concerned. Information on motorcycle parking is also available on the *www.motorcycleparking.com* website.

Other Types of Parking Bays

A range of parking bays are provided for specific

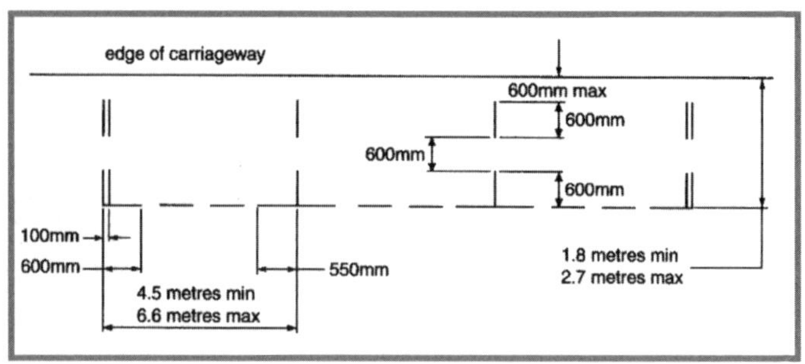

Individually marked parking bays.

categories of users including diplomats, ambulances, doctors, police etc. The most common are disabled persons' parking places. There are over 2 million disabled badge holders in the UK, many of whom are eligible for a disabled parking place outside their homes. Such is the demand that some councils simply mark the bay but do not make the traffic regulation order (TRO) to enable it to be enforced if a non-badge holder parks in the space. Bays that do have a TRO are also signed.

Parking 'places' and parking 'spaces'

A parking 'place' is a length of kerb defined in a parking places order where parking is permitted.

Within a parking 'place' there are parking 'spaces'. Most motorists understand that in meter or pay-and-display bays, where there is a maximum amount of time that a vehicle may stay, 'meter feeding' is not permitted. At the expiry of the paid for time the vehicle is required to leave and not return within a specified length of time.

However, what the parking places order will say is that a vehicle must not return to the same parking 'place' within a specified time after the expiry of the time paid for.

Aware of the fact that they must not 'meter feed', some motorists move their car to the next available space. Although they are parked in a different parking 'space' this is, unfortunately, often in the same parking 'place'. They are, therefore, in contravention of the parking places order and liable to be ticketed. In such circumstances you should either park in a different street, or in a bay on the opposite side of the street.

Permitted parking bays are becoming increasingly diverse. Some bays operate in excess of the hours of operation of the CPZ, while shared-use bays, that allow non permit holding visitors to park with a pay-and-display ticket during the operational hours of the CPZ, sometimes become

After 5 pm and on Sundays this 'shared use' bay is for residents only.

'permit holders only' bays in the evening and on Sundays. For these reasons it is more important than ever that motorists note what the signs indicate.

Key Cases

Posted on the Parking and Traffic Appeals Service website *www.parkingandtrafficappeals.gov.uk* are a selection of 'Key Cases'. For anyone considering an appeal it would be well worth while seeing if there is a similar case and finding out what the outcome was. If there is a similar case where the appeal was allowed you would do yourself no harm by drawing the adjudicator's attention to it.

Some of the cases are rather long and convoluted and, of course, written in legalese. Below is a summary of the findings on some of the more common issues.

Loading and unloading

Of all the many points of contention regarding parking the question of 'loading and unloading' must be at, or close, to the top of the list.

In the absence of any loading restriction, vehicles are allowed to wait to load and unload for so long

Those that appeal in person are slightly more successful than those who appeal by post!

as may be necessary for delivering or collecting goods at a premises adjacent to the street. If a parking attendant or traffic warden finds a vehicle parked on a yellow line without seeing any loading or unloading taking place a parking ticket will be issued. It is for the driver of that vehicle to demonstrate that he or she was loading or unloading, if that was the case, and that the ticket should be cancelled.

It is reasonable to expect that deliveries of smaller items should take less time than those of larger items and hence there would be a greater burden on the driver to justify a lengthy absence from the vehicle. The shorter the observation period of the parking attendant or traffic warden the better it will be for the motorist to claim that an exemption applies. Drivers making business deliveries will, in the majority of cases, be able to produce some form of documentation in the event of a ticket being issued.

There is no requirement that goods should be of a particular size or weight and the inclusion of postal packages within the definition of 'goods' suggests that it was the intention to include even comparatively small items.

A London adjudicator commented that a delivery in the course of trade or business falls more easily within the ordinary meaning of delivering goods, even if the size and weight is small. In the case of a milkman each delivery is of items small enough to be carried by hand but the vehicle is necessary for the delivery.

At first sight even a motorist doing his shopping might be able to claim to be 'loading'. However, choosing an item and chatting to a sales assistant could not properly be described as the collection or loading of goods. But a vehicle brought to a collection point to collect it would be exempt. Clearly it is impossible to arrive at a definition which leaves no room for argument.

In 1955 the High Court rejected that anyone merely putting into his car something bought from a shop was covered by the exemption. The motorist in question had purchased six champagne glasses. It was accepted that a car being used to collect bulky or heavy items would have been exempted.

The bigger the consignment and the bulkier the item the more time it is reasonable to expect to load and unload.

In a similar case in 1977 the appellant had parked his car whilst collecting wages. The High Court held that, although cash was covered in the definition of goods under the terms of the proviso, the real question that had to be addressed was whether the vehicle was used for the purposes of collection. On the facts, the court found that it was not. The driver had put the money in his pocket and merely used the car for convenience. It was he who collected the cash and not the vehicle.

Some local authorities state, incorrectly, that loading or unloading must be continuous, implying that there must be an uninterrupted movement of goods to or from the vehicle. This is unreasonable, as it is unrealistic to expect deliveries to be made without the checking of goods and paperwork as part of the delivery process. Difficulties arise where there are delays in this process.

In the case of Richard Few of the All London Cleaning Company, the appellant had been using a private estate car for the purposes of delivering cleaning materials. The vehicle was parked on a single yellow line in Westminster for five minutes, without any loading activity having been observed, and a PCN was issued. The appellant returned whilst the ticket was being issued. His appeal was allowed because, although the vehicle was not a commercial vehicle and five minutes had elapsed, the adjudicator was persuaded that the vehicle had been parked for no longer than was necessary to make the delivery.

However in another London case, a florist's van was also observed for a period of five minutes before a PCN was issued. Although there was a note on the dashboard 'florist making delivery' no evidence of loading/unloading was observed.

The adjudicator noted that there was no evidence on the precise size or nature of the flowers being delivered and it was, therefore, presumed to be a normal bouquet. The appeal was refused because there was no explanation why it should take five minutes to deliver a bouquet of flowers and the adjudicator was not satisfied that the vehicle was parked only for so long as was necessary to make the delivery.

A motorist left a van parked in a restricted street in Edinburgh for between 15 and 20 minutes whilst making a delivery. The delay was caused by having to wait for the parcel to be made up. The exemption covered 'for so long as may be necessary to enable goods to be loaded onto or unloaded from the vehicle'.

The Lord Justice Clerk said that the proviso covered not merely the acts of loading and unloading, in the narrow literal sense, but also the taking of the goods into those premises and putting them into some part of the premises. The driver had been away from the vehicle for a period of 12 minutes. Although a borderline case, the court was satisfied that during the period in question the process of loading and unloading was in fact being carried out.

However, in the case of an art dealer who parked his car for 35 minutes whilst he went to buy a picture, delay was caused by the assistant being unable to find the picture. The court found that whilst there was an exemption from the provisions of a no waiting order for loading and unloading the exemption did not extend to the leaving the vehicle for as long as might be necessary for the goods to be located.

That there should be so much confusion over this issue is not surprising bearing in mind the complexity of the law and the incorrect advice given in the Parking Attendants Handbook. As the London adjudicator, Edward Houghton, pointed out, the advice is incorrect in many instances. For instance it states that loading or unloading activity should be continuous, that vehicles should not be unattended and that goods do not include wages and small fragile items.

To be exempted from waiting restrictions you must demonstrate that the nature of the goods being delivered/collected required a vehicle to be used and to be parked adjacent to the delivery point. The bulkier the item and the bigger the consignment the more time it is reasonable to be allowed to load/unload. However, if you are ticketed whilst loading/unloading you must produce evidence to show this was, in fact, what you were doing.

Going for Change

When a motorist parks in a meter or pay-and-display bay, how much time is allowed to make the payment and does it include time to go for change? The answer can be seen from the verdicts of the following two cases.

In 1961 Mr Strong parked his car at a meter bay but had no change to pay. He went to get change but when he returned to his vehicle a few minutes later the vehicle had been ticketed. He refused to pay and was found guilty at a magistrates' court. He appealed to the divisional court but his appeal was dismissed.

The relevant order stated that the charge was 'payable on the leaving of the vehicle in the parking place'. The court held that 'no element of reasonable time can be imported at all unless it be such reasonable time as is involved in getting out of the driving seat and putting the coin into the meter. In other words, between stopping the car and stepping onto the pavement and inserting a coin'.

In 1981 Mr Hunt parked in a pay-and-display car park without having change. He went to get some and found a ticket on the vehicle when he returned a few minutes later.

On appeal, the court held that 'the latest time at which the charge must be paid is before the person parking the vehicle himself leaves the car park...It is simply not good enough to arrive at the car park without the appropriate coin and then to go off shopping with the intention of returning and paying the charge when your shopping expedition is complete.'

As these cases show, there is no concession to go for change and problems could arise whilst away from a vehicle to purchase a pay-and-display ticket. Ticket machines should be sighted so that they can be seen from any given pay-and-display bay and be no further than 30 metres from it. If the nearest machine is out of order, then the safest option would be to drive on and park in the vicinity of the next machine.

Pay-and-display

With pay-and-display there is an obligation to both 'pay' and 'display' the ticket during the time that the vehicle is parked. The instructions on the back of the ticket often ask the motorist to stick the ticket to the windscreen of the vehicle. Unfortunately, a tiny proportion of tickets purchased do not adhere to the windscreen for the duration of the time the vehicle is parked. When they fall they inevitably end up face down on the dashboard.

Less common is the case where tickets are displayed in open-topped cars and subsequently stolen by another motorist or removed by a child. In both cases the fee to park has been paid and the ticket displayed in accordance with the instructions. Understandably, motorists are much aggrieved when they return to their vehicle to find a penalty has been issued for failing to display a valid ticket.

Unfortunately appeals on these grounds have been refused by adjudicators.

Mr Carr parked his car and fixed the pay-and-display ticket on his windscreen in accordance with the instructions on the ticket. When he returned to the vehicle the ticket had fallen, face down, onto the dashboard and a PCN had been issued for failure to display a valid ticket.

The adjudicator accepted Mr Carr's account of events that he had purchased a ticket and displayed it as instructed. However, because the ticket came unstuck and fell face down on the dashboard, so that its details ceased to be visible from outside the vehicle, he was in contravention of the relevant regulations. For this reason the appeal was refused.

Mr Baker parked his open-topped car and fixed a ticket to the windscreen of his vehicle as instructed. When he returned to the vehicle the ticket was gone and a PCN had been issued. He appealed on the grounds that he had done everything he had been told to do and that he was blameless in this matter.

As with the Carr case the adjudicator accepted Mr Baker's version of events but, as before, Mr Baker was in contravention of the relevant regulations and his appeal was refused.

Mr Starkey's car was a kit car which had no side

windows. Like Mr Baker he purchased and displayed a ticket but somebody removed it after he left his vehicle and he was issued with a PCN.

The information on the ticket machine said that it was an offence to park without payment and display of ticket. The adjudicator said that reasonable motorists would read the words 'park without payment and display of ticket' as requiring them to display a ticket when they park and leave the vehicle. The words were not adequate to convey that if they have complied with that condition but the ticket is removed without their permission or falls down in some way so its details cease to be visible, then the liability will arise even where the ticket has not expired.

The adjudicator added: "Where a substantial penalty will be imposed, a specific warning must appear to make motorists aware of the importance of taking every possible step to ensure that the ticket remains visible at all times." The adjudicator recognised that in the case of a car such as the appellant's that might present practical difficulties, but said: "He must at least be put on notice of the risk he runs." The appeal was allowed.

This case was unusual in that it turned on the wording on the pay-and-display machine, which I am sure the council in question has since had changed! Pay-and-display machines usually have words to the effect that the ticket must be displayed at all times whilst the vehicle is in the parking place. Open topped cars are particularly vulnerable to having tickets removed. Given the cost of a parking fine it would be well worth the trouble of putting the hood up to avoid this from happening. If pay-and-display tickets are placed, face up, on the dash board the risk of tickets falling from the windscreen is also avoided.

Owner's Liability

Under the Road Traffic Act 1991, liability for parking tickets rests with the owner, and the owner is considered to be the registered keeper of the vehicle. This was challenged by a motorist, Miss Francis, whose vehicle received two parking tickets whilst it was with a garage for repair.

When she collected the vehicle there were no penalty charge notices on the vehicle, she was not told of them and was not aware of them until the NtOs arrived. She made representations to Wandsworth council in respect of each notice to the effect that she was not the owner of the vehicle at the time as she had given it to the garage for repair. The council rejected this representation so she took the matter to appeal which was upheld by the adjudicator. The Council challenged the decision of the adjudicator and took the case to a judicial review.

The council's case was that if a penalty charge is payable it is payable by the 'owner' of the vehicle and that the 'owner' was the 'registered keeper' as indicated on the vehicle registration document. The critical question was whether Miss Francis or the garage owner was the keeper of the vehicle at the material time.

Wandsworth's counsel argued that the disposal or acquisition of a vehicle referred to in the Act must be the sort that would require the notification of change of ownership. He said that this was not the approach of the Parking Adjudicator and if it had been he could not have concluded that merely entrusting the vehicle to the garage owner for repair amounted to a sufficient disposition to divest Miss Francis of the ownership which was hers by virtue of the registration.

The Court agreed and allowing the appeal said: "Clearly a sale or gift to another would satisfy the requirement but the keeper does not necessarily have to be the owner. The concept does, however, involve both a degree of permanence and the right to use the vehicle for the purpose for which it was manufactured, namely use on the road. Thus, a friend who borrows a car even for a comparatively long period would not as a rule become the keeper, nor would a garage proprietor who takes a vehicle for repair, since he has no right to use it for his own purposes and the duration of his possession of the car is insufficient. The whole concept of ownership for the purpose of this part of the 1991 Act is related to what is or what should be the position in the public record."

Footway parking

Public highway in urban areas is, invariably, made up of 'carriageway' and 'footway'. The limit of the carriageway is the kerb. Between the kerb and the premises fronting the highway is the footway. Carriageways are for the passage of vehicles, bicycles, handcarts and barrows and footways are exclusively for pedestrians unless specifically marked to the contrary. Strictly speaking a child on a tricycle or someone pushing a child in a buggy should not use the footway!

It would seem reasonable that vehicles should not drive on or otherwise encroach onto the footway.

However, with the volume of traffic and the narrowness of some carriageways, parking with two or more wheels on the footway is sometimes permitted.

In 1974, the Greater London Council banned parking with one or more wheels resting on a footway, central reservation or grass verge. Therefore, unless there are signs indicating the contrary, it is illegal for any vehicle to park in such a way within any London borough.

Outside London, councils wanting to prohibit footway parking must make a specific order. Where these powers are exercised, signs indicating the extent of the prohibition, must be erected. Thus in London you cannot park with wheels on the footway unless signs say you can. In the rest of the country you can park with wheels on the footway unless signs say you can't.

The same rules apply to motorcycles as cars. However, being small and manoeuvrable, bikes could often be parked in out-of-the-way corners and private forecourts without penalty. But in 2001 a London adjudicator ruled that although a scooter had been parked on pavement lights (the glass blocks set in a forecourt to allow light into a cellar), which was a private area, because pedestrians had unhindered access to the area it could be considered footway for the purposes of enforcement.

However, in Amery v Westminster City Council, the adjudicator said that pavement lights, draymen's doors, etc. may be within or without the building line; each case turns on its own facts. The appellant produced photographs that showed that the line included not only the pavement lights but

Motocycle parked on pavement lights

also steps to the door of the premises, a goods drop and stairs to the basement of other adjoining buildings. The appeal was allowed because the adjudicator found that the position of the scooter was within the building and did not form part of the public footway.

The chief adjudicator for the London Parking and Traffic Appeals Service says that there seems to be a common misconception that pavement lights are not part of the footway. This misconception seems to be the root of much of the problem. People should not assume that pavement lights are not part of the public footway and that therefore they can park on them.

He says: "Where the footway begins and ends is a matter of highway and road law, not parking law. As we have said, each case depends on its own facts. The only safe course is not to park on a given area unless it is quite clear that it is not part of the footway. I would be wary of parking anywhere that the public were not physically prevented from walking over, by a barrier of some kind such as a wall or fence. Of course, there are areas that are not physically separated that are not footway, but I would want to be absolutely clear about the position before parking in an 'open' area."

Councils' duty to act 'fairly'

The Road Traffic Act 1991 imposes a duty upon a local authority to act 'fairly'. This includes an obligation to take steps to enforce a parking penalty (e.g. by serving a Notice to Owner, or responding to representations) within a reasonable time. What will amount to a reasonable time will depend upon the individual circumstances of a particular case.

This means that a Notice to Owner should be served within 6 months of the issue of the Penalty Charge Notice upon which it is based. It is incumbent on a local authority to give the reason for the late issue of a NtO if this is not the case.

In exceptional cases, where additional time is needed to consider a representation, a council must show that the delay in considering the representations was not unreasonable.

Failure to enforce a parking penalty within a reasonable time breaches its obligation to act fairly. If an adjudicator finds that an authority has failed to comply with its duty to act fairly (for example, by failing to act with reasonable timeliness), he must allow the appellant's appeal.

If a vehicle is clamped or removed by a council the penalty charge and clamping or removal fees much be paid before the vehicle is released. A motorist may still challenge the validity of the parking ticket provided the challenge is made within 28 days of the issue of ticket. Where a representation to a clamping or removal is received by a council Section 71(6) of the 1991 Act requires that the council responds to the representation within 56 days of its receipt. If challenge is successful then both the penalty charge and the clamping or towing fee is refunded.

In the case of Montezemolo-v-Royal Borough of Kensington and Chelsea, Mr Montezemolo had made a representation to the council which he sent on 24 February 1998 and was received by the council on 27 February. The 56 day period therefore started on 27 February. The council responded to the representations in a letter dated and posted on 21 April which was received by Mr Montezemolo on 25 April.

The period of 56 days from 27 February 1998 ended on 23 April. That is two days after the Council posted its letter but two days before Mr Montezemolo received it.

The adjudicator said, in his view, section 71(6) of

the 1991 Act requires the Council's notice of its decision to be received by the person who has made representations within a certain time; that time is the period of 56 days beginning with the date on which the Council received the representations. As Mr Montezemolo was not served the council's response until the 58th day the appeal was allowed.

If you respond promptly to letters from the council and they either take a long time to respond, or fail to address the points that you put to them, the better the chance an adjudicator will take the view that the council has failed to act 'fairly'.

Validity of Penalty Charge Notices

Section 66(2) of the Road Traffic Act 1991says:

> For the purposes of this Part of this Act, a penalty charge is payable with respect to a vehicle by the owner of the vehicle…

Section 66(3) (c), (d) and (e) say:

(c) that the penalty charge must be paid before the end of the period of 28 days beginning with the date of the notice;

(d) that if the penalty charge is paid before the end of the period of 14 days beginning with the date of the notice, the amount of the penalty charge will be reduced by the specified proportion;

(e) that, if the penalty charge is not paid before the end of the 28 day period, a notice to owner may be served by the London authority on the person appearing to them to be the owner of the vehicle.

A challenge was made to a Wandsworth's PCN on the grounds that it did not comply with the above subsections. The PCN said: "...you are therefore required to pay the sum of £80 within 28 days." This did not comply with section 66 (2) because the person legally liable for payment of a penalty charge is the owner, who was not necessarily the driver at the time, and did not comply with section 66(3)(c) because it omitted to include "from the date of this notice". Similarly the advice regarding the discounted payment period failed to include "from the date of this notice".

The PCN said: "If no payment is received within 28 days of the date of issue, a Notice to Owner may be sent to the registered keeper of the vehicle requesting payment." This did not comply with section 66(3)(c) because again, the relevant period was incorrectly stated. The PCN referred to "the registered keeper" rather than "the person appearing to [the London authority] to be the owner of the vehicle", which did not comply with section 66(3)(e).

The Act places liability not on the registered keeper but on the owner. Although the owner was taken to be the registered keeper this is a rebuttable presumption. The local authority was empowered to serve a Notice to Owner on "the person who appears to them to have been the owner of the vehicle when the alleged contravention occurred", not on the registered keeper.

The Adjudicator said that literal compliance with the terms of section 66(3) was not essential. However, where a statute required a document to contain particular statements, the starting point for drafting a compliant document ought always be that the statutory language. This should be carried across to the document unless there were very good reasons for doing otherwise. Using the statutory language eliminated the opportunities for challenging the document for non-compliance. The statutory requirements took precedence over the commendable aim of couching documents in plain English. Local Authorities must be aware that the language they used, however plain, must bear the same meaning in substance as that prescribed by the statute.

Why things will only get worse!

There are several factors contributing to the transport, traffic and parking problems facing the UK today and the indications are that they are all getting worse!

Demographics

The number of drivers in Britain is likely to be determined by a mixture of economic, demographic and cultural factors. Of these demographics looks like being the major factor influencing the growth of drivers in the first quarter of the 21st century. For a variety of reasons the number of single person households will continue to rise. It has been estimated that every percentage point switch from multi to single person households could increase the number of cars by around 100,000.

However, the biggest demographic factor influencing the future number of cars on the road is the growth in the number of women with driving licences. Only a quarter of women over 65 have a driving licence, compared with nearly three quarters of men of the same age. But for women under 24 almost half have a driving licence. Lifestyle and employment opportunities for women suggest that they are likely to approach parity with men in the first quarter of the century. This could result in seven to eleven million additional cars on the road before 2020.

Public Transport

For many of those living away from conurbations public transport does not exist, and where it does it is infrequent and expensive. Within conurbations there is greater public transport provision, but even here the service it provides often leaves something to be desired. The situation is particularly bad in London and the south-east.

Transport for London admits that if the capital does not get an *extra* £15 billion to invest in rail improvements, the level of overcrowding will reach the level of some third world countries by 2011. London Underground is teetering on the point of collapse. The London Transport Users' Committee has complained to MPs that transporting animals in the conditions experienced by commuters on London Underground and commuter trains would not be allowed.

The congestion charging scheme introduced in London in 2003 reduced the number of vehicles entering central London by approximately 20% but the revenue raised has fallen below the levels predicted. Therefore investment in public transport infrastructure from congestion charging revenue is unlikely to have a significant effect in the short to medium term.

Government Policy

The government has made much of its desire to improve public transport, reduce road congestion and thereby entice motorists from their cars. But the signs are that the government is now giving up on being able to make any significant improvements to the many problems it faces. In 2000 it set a number of targets it wished to achieve by 2010. It wanted to:

- reduce congestion on motorways, trunk roads and large urban areas in England to levels below those prevailing in 2000
- improve rail punctuality and reliability with

a 50% increase in rail use from 2000 levels
- improve accessibility, punctuality and reliability of local public transport (bus and light rail) with an increase in use of more than 12% from 2000 levels.

Although the objectives remain, all the targets have now been dropped and, in respect of road congestion, the aim is only to reduce the rate of increase of congestion! The government also wants over two million new houses to be built by 2020, a disproportionate number of which will be in the south-east. Around London alone between 700/900,000 are proposed.

The residential parking problem

In 1993, the Transport Research Laboratory carried out a survey which sought to examine the future of parking in residential areas. The research showed that the number of cars parked on-street increased from 1.2 million in 1966 to 4.8 million in 1989. It was estimated that, taking account of the National Road Traffic Forecasts at that time and the likely increase in the number of dwellings, the number of cars parked on-street was likely to double between 1989 and 2025. In the light of events since 1993 this estimate is probably on the conservative side.

The opportunity to create additional parking spaces in residential areas is very limited. Approximately half the housing stock is either terraced houses or flats with no off-street parking. In seven out of the eight sites considered in the study, residents said that parking was a problem for them. Despite that, 18% said that they were intending to acquire additional vehicles in the next 12 months and fewer than 10% said that they would reduce the number of cars if problems increased.

When introducing parking schemes, some councils only allow one resident's permit per household, but the most do not impose such a restriction. There is a limit to the imbalance of permits to available bays beyond which parking schemes become ineffectual and public complaint will force councils to reassess their policies on permit issue.

Future scenario

The London congestion charging experiment has been more successful than its most enthusiastic proponents could have wished and it would be surprising if other cities do not introduce their own schemes. In conurbations there is very little on-street space either left uncontrolled or where provision is made for commuter parking.

Remaining uncontrolled streets are likely to be subject to controls in the not too distant future.

Demand for on-street paid for parking – meters and pay-and-display – will continue to be regulated through the price mechanism. The problem of uncontrolled demand for residents' parking will have to be addressed either by rationing permits or also through the price mechanism. Enforcement of parking restrictions by means of CCTV cameras is being used in London. It is cheaper, more efficient and there are fewer challenges to the tickets sent to motorists than those issued by parking attendants. It is reasonable to expect that camera enforcement will become the norm in the future – no one will be able to park illegally without getting a ticket!

Looking further into the future, the situation could arise where a parking space at your destination would have to be pre-booked. This would have a stabilising effect on traffic levels as only those with a parking space at their destination would take to the road. Thus the future looks to be one of greater regulation, more stringent enforcement and where parking spaces will either be rationed or restricted by price.

Keeping one step ahead – getting help

This book will help you challenge a parking ticket if you are unfortunate enough to get one and, hopefully, help you avoid one in the first place. However, the situation with regard to enforcement is constantly changing and the following websites have valuable information:

www.parkingticket.co.uk has loads of information and a lively bulletin board. There is a free monthly newsletter that gives the latest information about what is happening on the streets. You can subscribe to it from the site or by sending a blank e-mail to: parkingticket-subscribe@yahoogroups.com

www.parkingandtrafficappeals.gov.uk is the website of the London Parking and Traffic Appeals Service. In addition to other useful information it has a section on key cases it has considered. PATAS also deals with appeals on camera enforcement of bus lanes and Congestion Charging.

www.parking-appeals.gov.uk is the website of the

National Parking Adjudication Service. It deals with appeals outside London.

www.motorcycleparking.com, as its name suggests, specialises in motorcycle parking problems.

www.abd.org.uk is the website of the Association of British Drivers. It challenges current Government thinking that improvements in road safety are dependent on the installation of ever more speed cameras. The ABD believes that speed cameras are little more than revenue raisers for the Government and that improved road safety would be achieved by better driver training and education.

Glossary of terms

Additional Parking Charges

Charges imposed in addition to any initial charge for parking when motorists do not comply with parking controls. They include the penalty charge and charges for the release of clamped vehicles and for retrieving vehicles after they have been removed.

Adjudication

The final statutory opportunity for a motorist to contest a Penalty Charge Notice (and possibly the clamping and removal of a vehicle) through an appeal to an independent parking adjudicator. A motorist may only appeal after the council that issued the Penalty Charge Notice has rejected a formal representation and appeals may only made on certain, specified grounds. The decision of a parking adjudicator is final and binding on both parties to an appeal.

Authorisation Notice

The notice issued by a parking attendant to

indicate that a vehicle already issued with a Penalty Charge Notice is to be clamped or removed.

Certificated Bailiff
A bailiff authorised to recover parking debt. (In Scotland this is carried out by a Sheriff's Officer).

Charge Certificate
A notice issued to motorists who have received a Penalty Charge Notice and subsequent Notice to Owner but have not paid within the statutory time limit. A Charge Certificate increases the full penalty charge by 50% and requires payment within 14 days if registration of the debt is to be avoided.

Contravention
A failure by a motorist to comply with parking controls which have been decriminalised.

Controlled Parking Zone (CPZ)
An area where parking is restricted. Entry signs, placed on all vehicular entry points to the area, indicate the operational hours of the CPZ. The only signs within the zone will relate to the desig-

nated parking bays and any restrictions that are different from the CPZ hours.

Costs

A parking adjudicator has powers to award costs against either party to an appeal if in the opinion of the parking adjudicator either party has behaved in a "frivolous, vexatious or wholly unreasonable" fashion.

Debt Registration

An automated process of recording a parking debt with the Traffic Enforcement Centre at Northampton County Court. (In Scotland, after the expiry of the 14 days allowed for payment of the PCN after issue of the Charge Certificate, the certificate becomes the "extract registered decree arbitral" and has the same powers as a warrant, thereby allowing it to be passed to Sheriff Officers for recovery.).

Decriminalisation

Under the Road Traffic Act 1991, the Secretary of State for Transport can make Special Parking Orders, which allow councils to enforce contraventions of parking controls within a designated

Special Parking Area. Such contraventions are not criminal offences subject to a Fixed Penalty Notice, but are enforced through new, civil procedures. Thus they are said to have been "decriminalised".

Designated Parking Bays
Bays indicated by means of signs and white boxes on the carriageway for meter, permit, disabled badge holder parking, etc.

Discount Rate
A reduction in the penalty charge due if the Penalty Charge Notice is paid within 14 days of the date of issue.

Dispensation
An agreement to allow a vehicle to park in a restricted area, without penalty, for an agreed duration and without the need to pay any initial parking charge. Dispensations are issued by, or on behalf of, the council and an administrative charge may be made for this service. Dispensations are typically granted in limited circumstances where alternative provision cannot be made, for example, to enable work to take place at adjacent premises or for essential deliveries which will take longer

than the maximum time permitted.

DVLA
Driver and Vehicle Licensing Agency, based in Swansea.

Exemptions
Exemptions apply primarily to yellow lines and to the functions of loading, unloading and the picking up and setting down of passengers and their luggage. Certain classes of vehicle, e.g. emergency vehicles, are granted exemption from parking controls whilst on official business.

False Declaration
It is a criminal offence to "knowingly and wilfully" make an untrue statement in connection with an appeal to a parking adjudicator or at other stages in the enforcement process. Persons committing such offences risk conviction and a fine.

Fixed Penalty Notice (FPN)
Notices issued by police officers and police traffic wardens to motorists committing parking offences governed by criminal law. Police can also issued

FPNs in respect of a number of moving traffic offences.

Initial Charge
The basic charge set for parking in a designated parking bay, for specified users at specified times. Individual councils have responsibility for setting their own initial charges.

Loading Bay
A specific bay, bounded by white markings (red on Priority (Red) Routes in London) and signed to permit loading and unloading by goods vehicles. Parking is not permitted within these bays.

Loading Gap
An area of yellow line within a permitted parking place, on which waiting and parking is restricted but loading or unloading is allowed. Such gaps are considered to be permitted parking and are enforceable as such by councils.

National Parking Adjudication Service
An independent tribunal, created in 1999 to provide an independent adjudication service in

respect of Penalty Charge Notices issued in England (outside London) and Wales under the terms of the Road Traffic Act 1991.

Notice of Acceptance
A letter from a council to a motorist indicating that their formal representation against a Notice to Owner has been accepted.

Notice of Rejection (NoR)
A letter from a council to a motorist indicating that their formal representation against a Notice to Owner has been rejected.

Notice to Owner (NtO)
A statutory notice served by the council on the person believed by them to be the owner of a vehicle issued with a Penalty Charge Notice that remains unpaid after 28 days. On receipt of a Notice to Owner the owner must, within 28 days, either pay the fine or make a formal representation to the issuing council.

Notice of Appeal (NoA)
The form which must be issued to a motorist along with a Notice of Rejection which advises the

motorist of his right to appeal to an independent parking adjudicator.

Offence

Term used to describe a breach of the criminal law. Parking enforcement under the Road Traffic Act 1991 has been made a civil matter – thus the term "contravention" and not "offence" should be used in connection with decriminalised enforcement.

Order for Recovery

A statutory notice issued to the motorist notifying that an unpaid penalty charge has been registered as a debt at the Traffic Enforcement Centre at the County Court. (The procedure is different in Scotland).

Parking Adjudicator

An independent solicitor or barrister of at least five years professional standing, appointed under Section 73 of the Road Traffic Act 1991 to consider appeals against Penalty Charge Notices issued under the terms of that Act.

Parking Attendant (PA)

An appropriately qualified and trained officer

engaged by councils to issue Penalty Charge Notices. PAs may be employed direct by the council or through a specialist contractor.

Parking Bay/Space
An individual bay/space within a parking place that is provided for the leaving of a vehicle upon payment, or display of a permit or voucher as required.

Parking Place
Any area of highway where vehicles may legally be parked. A parking place may contain one or more parking bays or spaces. The end of a parking place will be denoted by double transverse lines.

Parking and Traffic Appeals Service (PATAS)
The adjudication service in London. In addition to parking appeals, PATAS also considers appeals in relation to bus lane contraventions and congestion charging in the capital.

Payment Centre
A place where motorists may pay any additional parking fines.

Penalty Charge Notice (PCN)
A notice issued by a parking attendant to a vehicle or to the person appearing to be in charge of a vehicle which is believed to be parked in contravention of the council's regulations.

Persistent Evaders
The term used for motorists who frequently incur Penalty Charge Notices and fail to make payment.

Persistent Offenders
The term used in respect of motorists who frequently receive Penalty Charge Notices but who do pay.

Pocket Book
A notebook used by parking attendants to record information while on duty. In particular, additional evidence to support Penalty Charge Notices issued during the course of their enforcement activities.

Pound
A secure place to which a removed vehicle is taken for storage until it is retrieved by the owner.

Priority Routes (Red Routes)
A network of major roads within London, specified by the Secretary of State as key roads where traffic flow is to be maintained. The Metropolitan Police retain responsibility for the enforcement of waiting and loading restrictions on red routes, although permitted parking is enforced by the council through whose area the red route runs.

Registered Keeper
The person or organisation recorded at the Driver and Vehicle Licensing Agency as being the keeper of a vehicle. Under the concept of "owner liability", councils may assume that the registered keeper is also the owner of the vehicle unless there is clear evidence to the contrary.

Review
Either party to an appeal can apply for a review of a parking adjudicator's decision. However, the grounds on which such an application may be made are extremely few.

Road Traffic Act 1991 (RTA 1991)
The Act of Parliament that decriminalised certain

parking offences, making them civil contraventions enforceable by local authorities.

Road Traffic Regulation Act 1984 (RTRA 1984)
The Act of Parliament which provided many of the powers for councils to introduce parking controls in their area.

Special Parking Area (SPA)
An area approved by the Secretary of State for Transport, within which the enforcement of most parking controls has been decriminalised and where enforcement may therefore be undertaken by the local authority.

Scottish Parking Appeals Service (SPAS)
The independent adjudication service in respect of Penalty Charge Notices issued within Scotland.

Statement of Liability
Part of the agreement signed by the hirer of a vehicle accepting that the hirer accepts liability in respect of Penalty Charge Notices issued to the

vehicle during the hire period. A hire agreement must contain the particulars required by the Road Traffic (Owner Liability) Regulations 2000 to enable the hire company to transfer liability in this fashion.

Statutory Declaration (England and Wales only)
A legal statement from a motorist in response to an Order for Recovery to the effect that an earlier stage in the enforcement process had not been complied with. A valid statutory declaration cancels the Charge Certificate and the associated 50% increase in the penalty charge and causes enforcement to revert to the NtO or appeal stage. It is a criminal offence to knowingly and willfully make a false Statutory Declaration.

Traffic Enforcement Centre (TEC)
Situated at Northampton County Court, this is the centre where unpaid penalty charges, in England and Wales, are registered as debts at the County Court.

Traffic Regulation Order (TRO)
An official order made by a local authority under

the Road Traffic Regulation Act 1984, which details the nature and extent of parking controls within the council's area. It is a contravention of these controls as detailed in a TRO that may give rise to the issuing of a Penalty Charge Notice. The same Orders are frequently known as Traffic Management Orders (TMOs) within London.

TRACE
The centralised inquiry line, run by the Association of London Government, in respect of vehicles removed by London boroughs.

Tribunal
An independent body created to provide a simple, accessible system of justice, allowing an appeal by the individual against administrative decisions made by the state. The National Parking Adjudication Service is one such tribunal.

Vehicle Registration Mark (VRM)
The number plate of a vehicle.

Vehicle Excise Disc (VED)
The tax disc of a vehicle. For enforcement purpos-

es, details of the serial number of the disc are recorded by the PA when issuing a PCN.

Waiver

A temporary consent, granted by the council, to relax parking controls for a specified vehicle or motorist.

Warrant of Execution

Authority issued by the county court to enforce an unpaid debt, following registration at the TEC. Warrants must be in the possession of a certificated bailiff when attempts are made to recover the debt.

Scotland does not have Bailiffs; instead, Sheriff Officer's carry out debt recovery. All remaining differences highlighted by the National Appeals Service are parts of a process not required in Scotland.

When a Charge Certificate becomes the "extract registered decree arbitral" it gives the Sheriff Officer thc legal right to "exercise diligence" (employ various methods of bebt recovery including wage arrestments, bank account arrestments etc.) on behalf of the Council.